Skills for Resolv

Team
Building

by

Marna Owen

GLOBE FEARON EDUCATIONAL PUBLISHER
A Division of Simon & Schuster
Upper Saddle River, New Jersey

Project Editors: Helene Avraham, Laura Baselice, Lynn W. Kloss
Executive Editor: Joan Carrafiello
Production Manager: Penny Gibson
Production Editor: Nicole Cypher
Marketing Manager: Marjorie Curson
Interior Electronic Design: Patricia Smythe
Illustrator: Donna Nettis
Photo Research: Jenifer Hixson
Electronic Page Production: Eric Dawson, Mimi Raihl
Cover Design: Eric Dawson
Cover Photo: Steve and Mary Beran Skjold

Reviewers:

Dorie L. Knaub, B.A., M.S.
Special Education Specialist
Downey Unified School District
Downey, California

Odalis Veronica Martin, B.A., M.S.
Special Education Teacher
Dade County Public Schools
Miami, Florida

Photo Credits: p. 4 © Lawrence Migdale; **p. 12:** © Richard Hutchings/Photo Researchers;
p. 14: Jeffrey High/Image Production; **p. 16:** © Radi Nabulsi; **p. 26:** Kathy Sloan/Photo
Researchers; **p. 28:** Radi Nabulsi; **p. 45:** Spencer Grant/The Picture Cube

Printed in the United States of America.   6 7 8 9 10 03 02 01

ISBN: 0-8359-1277-9

GLOBE FEARON EDUCATIONAL PUBLISHER
A Division of Simon & Schuster
Upper Saddle River, New Jersey

Contents

Chapter 1

What Makes a Dream Team?

Chapter Objectives

- Describe a team.
- List three reasons to work in teams.
- List four things that help a team work well.

Words to Know

team: two or more people who work together toward
    a common goal

purpose: goal or objective

accomplish (uh-KAHM-plish): to achieve

resolve (ri-ZAHLV): to work out or solve

When You Can't Do It Alone

Paul sat on an old tire in an empty lot. His
eyes scanned the trash-filled lot. People had
dumped all kinds of things there. Papers, old
furniture, rags, and broken machines littered
the ground. Once in a while, kids would try to
play among the rubble. All the broken glass,
however, made the area unsafe.

Julia, one of Paul's friends, stopped to talk.

"What are you staring at?" asked Julia.

"This place, it's a real dump!" said Paul.
"I'm sitting here thinking it would make a great
ball field. I wish I could clean it up."

Julia laughed. "It's useless. For every piece
of garbage you pick up, someone else will
throw another piece down."

Paul nodded. "I guess you're right. The job
is too big for me."

Julia looked thoughtful. "It's a good idea.
You would need a lot of help, though."

A smile spread across Paul's face. "What do
you say, Julia? You could be the first to join me.
Together, we could make this lot something to
be proud of."

What do you think of Paul's idea? If you lived in his neighborhood, would you join him?

_____

_____

What a Team!

Paul doesn't realize it, but he is starting a team. A **team** is a group of people who work together toward a common goal. Paul's team will work toward cleaning up the lot. Teams are sometimes called clubs, committees, or groups.

What makes any group a team is its **purpose**, or the reason it exists. A purpose is the team's main goal or objective. It brings the team together. It motivates the team members to work hard. By staying focused on the purpose, the team members are more likely to work through problems.

Listed below are different kinds of teams. Notice how each group of people became a team once they had a common purpose.

This group becomes a team...	When they agree to...
A family	plan a vacation.
Friends	raise money for a homeless shelter.
Co-workers at a job	pitch in to complete a difficult job.
A husband and wife	have a child and raise the youngster.
A health class	write a booklet on the dangers of drug use.

➤ What Makes It a Team?

Listed below are some types of teams. What do you think the purpose of each team might be?

1. A football team

_____

2. A group called "Save the Whales"

_____

3. A jazz band

_____

4. A school yearbook committee

_____

5. People who work in your school's main office

_____

➤ What's Your Experience?

Think about your own experience with teams. Describe a time when:

1. Your family acted as a team.

_____

_____

2. You and your friends acted as a team.

_____

_____

Why We Work in Teams

The more Paul and Julia talked about the project, the more excited they became.

"Just think, if we get a bunch of people together, we can really make a difference," said Paul.

"It will be more fun if we work together," said Julia.

Paul agrees. "If we pool our talents and knowledge, things around here could really change. There might even be less fighting around here!"

Paul and Julia are talking about some of the reasons people work in teams. For one thing, teams **accomplish** (uh-KAHM-plish), or achieve, more than one person could by working alone. Paul knows that he could never clean up the lot by himself. With the help of others, he can get much more done. For this reason, he and Julia plan to ask others to help work on the project.

Teams get more done for another reason. They make use of each team member's strengths. Paul is good at organizing people. However, he does not like to do physical work. Julia likes to do hard, physical work. Other team members will lend different strengths to the team. By pooling their skills and talents, the team will probably be successful.

Julia and Paul feel good about working toward a common purpose. They enjoy sharing their ideas. They are learning from each other. By working together, they are more creative and seem to have more energy.

Teams accomplish more than one person could.

Think about how a team might help each situation.

1. John doesn't like studying. He gets bored. "I can't stop myself from turning on the TV," he says. "I want to get good grades, but I can't do it alone!"

   What kind of team could John start or join? Why?

   \
   \

2. Marty wants to enter a fashion contest. She is very good at designing clothes. On paper, her outfits look great. She's not very good at sewing, though, and her clothes never look like her designs.

   What kind of team could Marty start or join? Why?

   \
   \

What Makes a Dream Team?

Paul and Julia were having a good time planning how their team would clean up the vacant lot. One day, Julia stopped being so excited.

"You know, I've been on some pretty crummy teams," she said. "I hated the field hockey team. All the coach did was yell. I also disliked being a member of the School Improvement Team. Nobody listened to me, so I quit. How will our team be different?"

Paul stopped and thought. "Well, we'll have to run our team so that those things don't happen. If we plan ahead, we can stop problems before they start."

Julia made a good point. Not all teams run smoothly. Not all team members find the experience enjoyable and rewarding. But, with a little planning, any team can be a dream team. Here are four things that most dream teams have in common.

1. **A Team Plan.** A team must have a clear purpose. It also needs a good plan to achieve that purpose. A clear plan keeps things on track. It enables team members to use their energy and skills in the best possible way.

2. **Team Trust.** A team works best when its members trust each other. When there is trust, people can learn from each other. This helps the team members to be more creative.

3. **A Way to Make Decisions.** On a dream team, everyone knows and agrees upon the way decisions are made. Each member has some say in the decision-making process.

4. **A Way to Resolve Problems.** Whenever people work together, there will be problems. Members may disagree on how to do things. They may dislike each other and have difficulty working together. A dream team knows how to **resolve** (ri-ZAHLV), or work out, such problems. Team members do not let problems stop the team from reaching its goal.

Thinking ahead can help teams prevent problems.

➤ Team Builder

Every team needs a set of rules that the members agree to follow. Check the rules below that you think would help create a dream team.

_____ Members must be on time for all meetings.

_____ The team leader makes all decisions.

_____ Every member gets a chance to speak.

_____ Every member gets a chance to share ideas.

_____ All members must agree to every decision made.

_____ Members who miss a meeting are kicked out.

_____ The team leader should never be questioned.

_____ All team members receive equal respect.

➤ Team Exercise

Show your list to a classmate. Do you agree on what would make a dream team? Talk over your differences. See if you can come up with a list of rules that you agree upon. Write them below.

_____

_____

_____

_____

_____

_____

_____

Think about a team that you have belonged to. Was your team a dream team? If not, what things were missing from your team?

_____

_____

Building a Dream Team

As you work through this book, you will discover how to build your own dream team. You will learn how to be a productive team member and a positive team leader. Are you ready to get into the team spirit?

Imagine that you are starting a team. Answer the following questions about your team.

1. What is the purpose of your team?

_____

_____

2. Why would people want to belong to your team?

_____

_____

_____

3. List four rules for your team. Explain why you chose each rule.

_____

_____

_____

_____

_____

_____

_____

_____

_____

_____

Chapter Summary

- A team is any group of people who work together with a common purpose.
- Teams accomplish more than one person could working alone. A team takes advantage of its members' different skills and talents. By working together, team members are more creative and learn from each other.
- Teams that work well have four things in common: a clear plan, trust, a set way to make decisions and resolve problems, and a set of rules that helps them to run smoothly.

Chapter Review

Words to Know

Match each word on the left to its meaning on the right. Write the correct letter in the space provided.

_____ **1.** accomplish   **a.** goal or objective

_____ **2.** purpose   **b.** to work out

_____ **3.** resolve   **c.** to achieve

_____ **4.** team   **d.** people working together for a common goal

About Teams

1. Give an example of a team. Explain its purpose.

_____

_____

2. What are three reasons people work on teams?

_____

_____

_____

3. What are the four things that most dream teams have in common?

_____

_____

_____

_____

Chapter 2

Team Planning

Chapter Objectives

- List two reasons for involving team members in team planning.
- Describe three parts of a team plan.
- Identify rules commonly followed by dream teams.

Words to Know

volunteer (vahl-uhn-TEER): to offer services free of charge or of one's own free will

approval: the act of agreeing or giving consent to

outcomes: the things you want to achieve

progress: to move toward a goal

What Do We Do Next?

Paul and Julia walked through their neighborhood. They told people about their idea for cleaning up the lot. "Come join us," they said. "As a team, we can make it happen!"

They invited everyone to a meeting at six o'clock that evening. Eight people said that they would definitely attend the meeting. A few others said that they might show up. Several people simply laughed at the idea.

"I guess we're lucky to get eight people to agree to come to the meeting," said Julia. "What are we going to do with them? Send everyone into the lot to pick up garbage?"

Paul was thinking. "I wish it was that easy. I think it would be better if we start with a plan."

"Oh, good idea," said Julia. "You go figure out a plan. Then, at the meeting tonight, you can tell us what to do."

Paul shook his head. "No, I think we'll use the meeting as a planning session. I want to hear everyone's ideas of how we should go about fixing up the lot."

"OK," said Julia. "But I don't see the point. Why don't you just tell us what to do?"

Why do you think Paul wants everyone to help with the plan?

_____

_____

On a team, everyone's voice should be heard.

How a Team Plans

Every team needs a plan. The plan tells the team where it wants to go. It also tells the team how to get there.

There are different ways to come up with a team plan. On some teams the leader makes the plan. The leader then tells the team members what to do. That is a simple way of doing things. But, it is not always the best way to make a plan.

Paul remembers the old saying, "Two heads are better than one." That is why he has decided to ask others to help make the team plan. Team members might have important ideas that they would not think of alone. By having all the members express their ideas, the team plan will be stronger.

There is another reason why Paul wants to involve the team members. When team members give their ideas and agree to a plan, they feel as if they own the plan. It becomes their plan, not just the team leader's plan. They believe in the plan. They work harder to make it a reality.

How can a dream team get everyone involved? That depends upon the size of the team. Small teams can have members where everyone **volunteers** (vahl-uhn-TEERZ), or offers, ideas. Larger teams might ask team members for ideas. A few members, or the team leader, can make a plan from the ideas given. The final plan then goes before the entire team for **approval**, or final agreement.

In later sections of this book, you will be provided with more ways for getting team members' ideas and making team decisions. For now, remember that a team's plan is strongest when all members help to make it.

➤ Team Builder

Suppose that you decide to have a party with three of your friends. Each of you agrees to contribute equal amounts of money to cover the cost of the party. One friend takes the money and then tells the rest of you what to do. This friend never asks any of you for ideas about the party.

1. How do you feel about the party?

_____

_____

2. How do you feel about the way your friend handled things? What could your friend have done differently?

_____

_____

_____

_____

3. Write four ideas about your plan for the party.

_____

_____

_____

_____

4. Compare your ideas for the party's plan with those of a classmate. Did your classmate think of something that you didn't think of including in your plan? Add it below.

_____

_____

A Team is Born

Paul, Julia, and eight people from the neighborhood attended the first team meeting. Paul started the meeting.

"Welcome," he said. "As you know, we're here to talk about cleaning up the vacant lot. I thought we'd use this meeting to plan how to go about the project."

"Wait a minute," said one person. "I thought we were here to get the city to clean up the lot."

Another person spoke up. "I thought we were forming a baseball team."

"I don't play baseball," said another. "I just want to do something about the lot. I just hate the way it looks."

Paul held up his hands. "Since we're a brand new team, let's begin by talking about what we want to do. Then, we'll discuss how to get it done. That will be our plan."

Begin with the Purpose

Paul is right. The first step in forming a team plan is having all the team members agree on the team's purpose. Paul asked every team member for ideas. The team looked at the ideas and talked about them. Finally, they wrote a team purpose statement that everyone agreed with. The members even agreed on a team name! At the end of the meeting, the team's purpose statement was:

"We call ourselves LIP, the Lot Improvement People. Our purpose is to turn the empty lot on 43rd Avenue into something that everyone in our neighborhood can use and will take care of."

➤ Team Builder

Work with three classmates to write a purpose statement that you all agree with. To begin:

1. Make a list of problems or issues in the school or neighborhood that you would like to fix. Write down all of the ideas suggested.

_____

_____

_____

_____

2. Identify one problem from the list that all of you would like to work on.

_____

3. Write a purpose statement for your team that describes your purpose or goals. Be sure that all team members agree.

_____

_____

Writing Team Goals

The LIP team continued their plan. They realized that there was a lot they needed to learn. Who owned the lot? Would the city help their project? Could they put play equipment on the lot? Could they make it into a ball field?

The team wrote down a list of goals. The goals were **outcomes**, or things they wanted to achieve. This is what the LIP team came up with:

- Find people in the city government who will help us.
- Get the owner of the lot to help us.
- Ask other members of the community for ideas about how to use the lot.

Can you add to this list of goals?

The team agreed that they would make more plans once they had this information.

➤ Team Builder

Look over the purpose statement you wrote with classmates in the previous exercise. Write three goals to include in your team plan.

_____

_____

_____

The Plan Continues

Once the team had identified its goals, Paul asked for volunteers to work on each goal. At first, no one said anything. Then Julia spoke up. "My brother sells property. Maybe he could help me find out who owns the lot. I could call the person and describe our plan. I'll need at least two weeks to get this done."

Two other team members volunteered to poll people in the neighborhood to see how they'd like the lot to be used. While conducting the poll, they would tell people about LIP and ask for their help.

Another team member agreed to call the city. He was in a government class at school and thought that his teacher might be able to help contact the right people.

"That sounds like something I'd like to learn about," said Paul. "Maybe I could help you."

After each team member had an assignment, they set dates to have each task completed by. The plan was finished! The members shook hands and went on their way.

If you were a LIP team member, what would you want to work on?

Who Does What By When?

The final part of any team plan is deciding who is responsible for each task and when the task should be completed. The LIP team accomplished this by:

1. Team members each chose a goal to work on. They based their choice on their interests, their strengths, or what they wanted to learn.

2. Team members broke their goals down into smaller steps. By doing this, their goals did not seem too huge or too hard to achieve.
3. They set dates for having things done. Dates keep people moving and on track. Deadlines help the team **progress**, or move toward a goal.

➤ Team Builder

Look at the three goals you wrote in the previous exercise. Identify two goals you would like to work on. Break each goal down into smaller steps.

Goal 1: _____

   Step 1: _____

   Step 2: _____

   Step 3: _____

Goal 2: _____

   Step 1: _____

   Step 2: _____

   Step 3: _____

Why did you choose these goals? _____

_____

Sunday	Monday	Tuesday	Wednesday	Thursday	Friday	Saturday
		1	2 Paul— call the Mayor	3	4	5
6	7	8	9	10 Kiko— call Real Estate office	11	12
13	14	15 Julia — Find out who owns lot	16	17	18	19
20	21	22	23	24	25 Lyle + Kiko— poll people in neighborhood	26
27	28	29	30	31		

➤ **Planning Rules**

Look at the list of rules below. Check the rules that you think a team should have.

_____ All team members must agree on the team's purpose.

_____ All planning is done by the team leader alone.

_____ Team members take part in all planning.

_____ Each team member has a role in achieving the team goal.

_____ The team leader is responsible for accomplishing all goals.

_____ Team members are allowed to work at their own pace.

_____ Team members identify dates for completing their tasks and must keep these dates.

Chapter Summary

- All team members should be involved in team planning. By taking part in the planning, members believe in the plan and work harder to carry it out.

- A good team plan includes: a team purpose statement that states why the team exists; goals or things that the team wants to achieve; and steps for each goal with dates for accomplishing each step.

- A strong team involves its members in the planning process. Its team members believe in the team's purpose and help in achieving the team's goals.

Chapter Review

Words to Know

Match each word on the left to its meaning on the right. Write the correct letter in the space provided.

_____ **1.** approval   **a.** to move toward a goal

_____ **2.** outcomes   **b.** to offer services freely

_____ **3.** progress   **c.** things you want to achieve

_____ **4.** volunteer   **d.** giving consent or agreeing

About Team Plans

In the space provided, write **T** if the statement is true or **F** if the statement is false.

_____ **1.** The saying "Two heads are better than one" is true for team planning.

_____ **2.** Team members work hardest on a plan that the team leader makes alone.

_____ **3.** A team's plan should begin with its purpose.

_____ **4.** Goals are not included in a team plan.

_____ **5.** Each team member should complete a task that helps the team reach its goal.

Getting Personal

Think about a team you belong to. How could you be a better team member?

_____

_____

Chapter 3

Team Trust

Chapter Objectives

- Explain why it is important for teams to have trust.
- Describe three ways to build trust.
- Identify team rules that help build trust.

Words to Know

trust: to rely on or have confidence in
criticize: to make fun of, or to judge
brainstorming: offering many ideas
communicate: to send and receive messages
commitment: to promise to do something

Don't Everybody Talk at Once!

Paul began the second meeting of LIP, the Lot Improvement People.

"OK," he said. "What did you find out? What did you accomplish?"

There was a long silence.

Finally, a member of the team named Lyle spoke up. "Well, I'll tell the team what I did if you all agree not to tell me I did a lousy job!"

Paul was surprised at this remark. "Sure, Lyle," he said. "You have my promise. How about the rest of you? Can we agree that we'll respect what Lyle has to say?"

Only after the team members nodded their heads in agreement, did Lyle begin to speak.

➤ What Do You Think

Why were the members afraid to speak?

_____

_____

_____

Trust on Teams

Lyle was reluctant to speak because trust was missing from the LIP team. When you **trust** people, you feel that you can rely on them or have confidence in them. You are able to share things easily because you know you won't be judged, or made fun of.

It is important to have trust on a team. Trust helps the team in many ways. When there is trust, team members are more willing to be creative. They know that they won't be made fun of even if their ideas seem strange or unusual. Trust also makes team members feel relaxed.

Trust helps the team get more work done. Team members don't worry about what others think. They concentrate on their goals. They are more likely to ask each other for help and learn from each other.

Team trust does not happen by accident. It is built by the words and actions of team members and the team leader. Each member of the team helps team trust to grow.

What kinds of things destroy trust?

➤ ## Where Does Trust Come From?

Think of a person whom you trust. What does that person do or say that causes you to trust him or her?

_____

_____

_____

All Ideas are Good Ones

The LIP team was making a list of the ways that the vacant lot could be used. Paul began the discussion.

"I want to hear everyone's thoughts about how the lot should be used. I'll write the ideas on this sheet of paper. Before we begin, we have to agree that all ideas are good ideas. No one is allowed to **criticize**, or make fun of, anyone's comments. Do we all agree?"

Everyone agreed.

"Great," said Paul. "We'll do this for 20 minutes. Now let's get started."

Team members volunteered ideas faster than Paul could write them down. In a short time, the paper was filled!

Building Trust Through Brainstorming

The LIP team used **brainstorming**, or the offering of many ideas, to list some ways that the lot might be used. In this process, one idea is as good as the next. This makes team members feel that their ideas are valuable in some way. They feel they have a safe place to voice their ideas, no matter how unusual they might be. For brainstorming to build trust, a team should follow Paul's example:

Brainstorming is one way to build trust.

- All ideas are good ideas. Ideas should not be judged as good or bad.
- Listen to all ideas. Sometimes, one idea will help you to think of additional ideas.
- Every idea is written down.
- A time limit is set for the session.

1. How many different ways could you use an empty shoe box? List all of the possible uses you can think of in one minute.

_____

_____

_____

_____

2. Compare your list with the list of a classmate. How many different uses are on your classmate's list? Write them below.

_____

_____

_____

3. What are some advantages to brainstorming with others rather than by yourself? Write them below.

_____

_____

Here's What Happened

After the meeting, Julia came up to Paul. "I really have to hand it to you," she said.

"Why?" replied Paul.

"Those brainstorming rules were great," said Julia. "The group is really starting to work together as a team."

"Thanks," said Paul. He was glad to have Julia as a team member.

Building Trust with Open Communication

Julia's comment built trust between Paul and her. Team leaders and team members can show and build trust by communicating openly. When you **communicate**, you send and receive messages with another person. In the case of the LIP team, Julia noticed that Paul had done something well. She told Paul what she liked and why she liked it. Her few simple words made Paul feel good. The trust between them grew.

Here are some ways that you can build trust with team members through open communication:

- Give positive comments when someone does something well. Tell the person what was good and why you liked it.
- Listen to others with an open mind. If you don't agree with what the person is saying, ask for more information. Say "Tell me more" instead of "I don't think that would ever work."
- Stay away from gossip or negative, chatty talk. Gossip destroys trust between people. If you have a problem with someone, go to that person and try to work things out.
- Agree to disagree with members of your team. Disagreeing with each other should be seen as an opportunity for solving problems.

Positive comments encourage people to speak their minds.

Below is a list of statements that team members might say to each other. Decide whether each statement would open or close communication. Mark the statements that open communication with an *O* and those that close communication with a *C*.

_____   **1.** "I've never heard of such a stupid idea."

_____   **2.** "Get real. That will never work."

_____   **3.** "I really liked the way you wrote this letter. Good work!"

_____   **4.** "Did you see what she did? She's ridiculous!"

_____   **5.** "I like that idea. Here's another way to look at it."

_____   **6.** "Jon, I have a problem with the way this was done. Let's talk about it."

_____   **7.** "I'm not sure I understand what you mean. Tell me more."

_____   **8.** "His ideas are awful! I don't know why we ever let him join this team!"

_____   **9.** "I disagree. This is how I think we should do it."

_____   **10.** "Thanks for being on time."

You Can Count on Me

Lyle, one of LIP's team members, was watching Julia draw a plan for the vacant lot.

"You can really draw well," said Lyle. "I can't even draw a stick figure!"

Julia smiled. "Thanks. But I wouldn't be drawing anything if you hadn't made so many phone calls. Think about all the work you've done! You have a way with words that I only dream of!"

Lyle laughed. "One of the things I like about this team is watching and learning from others. The other thing I like is knowing that my team members will do what they say they will do."

"Me, too," said Julia. "What we're doing together makes me feel good."

Building Trust Through Commitment

A good team will always accomplish more than one person working alone. This is because team members have different strengths. Think about any sports team. Some players are known for their strength. Others are quick-thinkers. Still others have leadership skills that pull the team together.

Team members rely on each other's strengths. For trust to grow, team members must recognize and appreciate each other. They must also keep their **commitments**, or promises. When a team member doesn't do his or her job, trust breaks down. Being on time for meetings is one simple way to build trust. It shows commitment to the team. Another way to build trust is to go to team members for help. This shows that you value and trust another's strengths. A third way of building trust is to offer help when others need it.

What are some of your strengths?

In order to complete this activity, you need to work with three classmates that you don't know very well. Begin by reading the passage. Then, answer the questions in the space provided.

Imagine you were in a plane crash. You and your classmates are the only survivors. It's snowing, very cold, and dark outside.

1. What would each of you do to help the group survive the night?

_____

_____

_____

_____

2. How would you feel if one person didn't keep his or her commitment? Would you be more or less likely to trust the others?

_____

_____

_____

_____

3. Suppose each person kept his or her commitment. What effect would this have on the trust between the members of the group?

_____

_____

_____

➤ Rules for Trust

Check the rules that you think will help a team build trust.

_____ Team members must respect each other's ideas.

_____ Only good ideas are welcome.

_____ Gossip is not allowed.

_____ Disagreement is an opportunity for new ideas.

_____ Team members who cannot work out problems should quit the team.

_____ All members should be on time for meetings.

_____ All members must keep their commitments.

What rules would you add to this list? _____

Chapter Summary

- Team trust helps team members to be more creative, to have more fun, and to get more work done.
- Team trust can be built by listening to everyone's ideas without judgment. Open communication also helps to build trust.
- In a strong team, all ideas are welcome while gossip is avoided. Members are allowed to disagree with each other. All members arrive on time to meetings and keep commitments. Members who cannot work out problems bring them to the team leader.

Chapter Review

Words to Know

Complete each statement with a word listed below.

criticize　　　　commitment　　　　trust

communicate　　brainstorming

1. When you promise to do something, you are making a_____.

2. The group made a list of ideas by _____.

3. When you judge, you _____.

4. People you rely on are people you can _____.

5. You _____ when you send and receive messages.

Ways to Build Trust

Circle the statements below that build team trust.

1. All ideas are good ideas.

2. When team members disagree, they should say so.

3. Team members should not care if others are late for meetings.

4. Team members should use their strengths to help each other.

5. When brainstorming, people should hesitate to offer ideas.

Getting Personal

What are two things you can do today to help build trust? _____

_____

Chapter 4

Team Decisions

Chapter Objectives

- Identify three ways to make decisions.
- Explore how to get a consensus on a decision.
- Describe team rules for making decisions.

Words to Know

vote: to express a choice
majority: the greater part or larger number
consensus (kuhn-SEN-suhs): agreement

What Do We Do Now?

The LIP team had accomplished a great deal. They had found the owner of the vacant lot. The owner agreed to sell the lot to the city. When the city said it didn't have any money available to buy the lot, the LIP had to come up with another plan. They decided to contact a local newspaper and see if they would run the story. A wealthy citizen saw the story, bought the lot, and donated it to the city. LIP's next task was to decide how to use the lot. Their decision would go to the city for final approval.

At a team meeting, Paul posted the list of possible uses for the lot that the team had already thought of. There were too many good ideas included on the list.

"Well, how do we pick the best idea?" asked Julia.

"Let's vote," said someone.

"No, let Paul decide. He's the team leader," said another member.

Someone else spoke up. "Wait a minute. There are a lot of great ideas up there. I think we should talk about it and choose the one that we all agree is the best."

Paul stared at the list. Then he shook his head. "I would say the first thing we have to do," he said, "is decide how to decide."

What do you think is the best way for a team to make a decision? Why?

_____

_____

_____

How Do We Make Good Decisions?

All teams want to make good decisions. A good decision is one that is carefully thought out, that chooses the best option, and that all team members support.

There are many ways a team can make decisions. Each way has pros, or reasons for it, and cons, or reasons against it. Teams may decide to use one way, or a variety of ways to make a decision. The important thing is that the entire team decides *how* to decide.

➤ **How Do Decisions Get Made?**

The teams that you belong to make decisions all the time. Describe how each of the following teams makes an important decision.

1. How are decisions made within your family?

_____

_____

2. How are decisions made among your friends?

_____

_____

3. How are decisions made in a classroom?

_____

_____

Three Ways to Make Decisions

The LIP members suggested three different ways of deciding how to use the lot. Let's look at the advantages and disadvantages of each method.

1. Let the Team Leader Decide!

This is the way many teams operate. The team leader gets ideas or information. Sometimes, the leader discusses things with the team. Other times, the leader reviews the information alone. Either way, the team leader makes the final decision alone.

Letting the team leader make the decision has its good points. It's very useful in emergencies when there is no time for a lengthy discussion. But there is one problem with this method of decision-making. The final decision might not be one that the rest of the team agrees with. As a result, the team may not work as hard to see the decision carried out.

2. Let's Take a Vote

Taking a **vote**, or having each team member express a choice, is another way to make a team decision. Several options are offered to team members. The members vote either for, or against, each option. The option that gets the most, or the **majority**, of votes wins.

This method can be a quick way to make a decision. Since a majority of team members have to agree on the decision, it will have a lot of support. However, team members who voted for a different option may feel disappointed. Voting can put team members in competition with each other. It can cause some team members to be unhappy.

3. Get Agreement from All Team Members

Another way to make a decision is to get all of the team members to agree on the best decision. This is called reaching a **consensus** (kuhn-SEN-suhs), or agreement. Reaching a consensus can be a slow process. Team members must talk things over, think about their options, and persuade each other. It is often difficult to get a large number of people to reach an agreement.

However, many teams reach decisions through consensus. In this process, all team members are involved. They know that their input matters. They offer ideas, think creatively, and listen to each other. Since the entire team supports the final decision, members work harder to carry it out.

When team members reach a consensus, everyone wins.

➤ Team Builder

Complete this activity with four classmates. Begin by selecting a team leader.

Imagine you will be selling ice cream cones at a fair to raise money for a local charity. A local ice cream shop will donate three kinds of ice cream. Your team must select three of the following flavors to sell at the fair:

vanilla   chocolate chip   cookies & cream

chocolate   pistachio   cookie dough

strawberry   fudge swirl   cherry vanilla

1. First let the team leader make the decision alone. Identify the choices.

   _____

   _____

   _____

2. Now take a vote to decide which flavors to sell. Team members should write their three choices on a slip of paper. What flavors received the greatest number of votes? _____

   _____

   _____

3. Now try to reach a decision by consensus. Limit your discussion to ten minutes. What flavors did all team members agree to? _____

   _____

   _____

Making Consensus Work

The LIP team decided that they wanted to reach a consensus on how to use the lot. They talked and talked. When the discussion was over, they had finally come to an agreement.

Reaching consensus can be hard work. It helps to have a team leader lead the discussion. Here are some steps the leader can follow:

1. The team leader describes the decision that has to be made.

2. All members of the team offer possible options.

3. All members take turns saying what they think is the best option and why they fee this way. No one is allowed to interrupt a speaker.

In the world of team building, taking turns is called *round robin.*

4. Repeat Step 2. Some members may have changed their minds.
5. Open up the discussion. Members listen to each other's viewpoints and make their choices.
6. When everyone agrees on a decision, consensus is reached!

The Great Ice Cream Decision

Following is an example of how this process was used to decide which ice cream flavors to sell at the fair.

Step 1: Describe the Decision.

Team Leader: "OK. We have nine flavors to choose from. The store will only donate three. We're here to choose the three that will sell the best."

Step 2: Brainstorm Choices.

Team Leader: "Here are our choices." The list of nine flavors was shown to the rest of the team. "Are there any other options?"

Team Member: "Yes, I think we should get donations from another ice cream shop."

Team Member: "We might try asking the store to donate additional flavors."

Step 3: Let Each Member Have a Say.

Team Member: "I think we should choose chocolate, vanilla, and strawberry. Everybody likes those flavors. They are safe choices."

Team Member: "I think chocolate and vanilla are good choices. Everyone likes those. But, I think we need to include a more exciting flavor. Maybe cookie dough. Little kids love it, and so do I!"

Team Leader: "OK. We have an agreement about vanilla and chocolate. Let's talk about the third flavor."

Step 4: Let Each Member Have a Say (Again).

Team Member: "I like the idea of going with a more exciting flavor. Cookie dough is fine with me."

Team Member: "Great! I agree!"

Step 5: Open Up the Discussion.

Team Leader: "What about going back to the ice cream store and asking for more flavors? Are we sure we want to abandon that idea?"

Team Member: "We don't have much time left before the fair begins. I think it's a good idea to make our choices now."

Team Member: "I agree."

Step 6: Agreement!

Team Leader: "OK. We all agree that the three flavors we will sell at the fair are chocolate, vanilla, and cookie dough. Good work!"

➤ Team Builder

Get together with your ice cream team. Your next task is to decide which two-hour block of time is best for selling ice cream. Your choices are:

2 PM to 4 PM   4 PM to 6 PM   6 PM to 8 PM

Have your team leader lead the discussion. Use the steps for reaching a consensus to make your decision.

What was your team's decision? How did you feel in the decision-making process?

_____

_____

_____

➤ Rules for Making Decisions

Check the rules that you think will help a team make a decision.

_____ All team members should help make the decision.

_____ The team leader should make decisions when there is an emergency.

_____ All members respect each other's ideas.

_____ No one is allowed to interrupt a speaker.

_____ Disagreement is an opportunity for new ideas.

_____ Once a team has made a decision, all team members must support it.

Are there any rules you would add to this list? Write them below.

_____

_____

Chapter Summary

- Three common ways of making a decision are letting the team leader decide, taking a vote, and reaching consensus or agreement.
- Getting consensus on a decision takes time. It helps to: (1) state the decision, (2) identify the choices, (3) let everyone state his or her reasons for the choice, (4) identify choices again, (5) open the discussion, and (6) reach an agreement.
- For any team decision to work, all team members must understand and agree on how the decision will be made. Team members must agree to support the decision.

Chapter Review

Words to Know

Match each word on the left to its meaning on the right. Write the correct letter in the space provided.

_____ **1.** consensus   **a.** greater part or larger number

_____ **2.** vote   **b.** agreement

_____ **3.** majority   **c.** to express a choice

About Team Decisions

Complete the table below.

Way to Make Decisions	Advantage	Disadvantage
Team Leader Decide		
Vote		
Consensus		

Getting Personal

Which method of making a decision do you like best? Explain.

_____

_____

Chapter 5

Resolving Team Conflict

Chapter Objectives

- Describe some of the causes of team conflict.
- Practice skills for resolving team conflict.
- Identify rules for resolving team conflict.

Words to Know

conflict: disagreement due to different goals or
    interests; to clash

What Went Wrong?

LIP had successfully cleaned up the vacant
lot. It now was a wide, green field used for
playing sports. On one side of the field was a
play structure for young children. On the other
side of the field were benches and tables where
people could play chess.

On the day the lot was to be dedicated by
city leaders, Paul gathered the team together
at his house. "Before we go to the celebration,"
began Paul, "I want to say that each one of you
is great! You really worked together to make a
wonderful team! Now, does anyone have
anything to say before we leave?"

Julia raised her hand. "Yes. I'm not going to
the celebration." She stared at Kiko, another
member of the team. "I have my reasons."

"Good," said Kiko. "It will be better without
you there."

Paul's mouth dropped open. They had
come so far and accomplished so much! What
had happened?

> ### ► Think About It

If you were Paul, how would you handle this situation? Why?

_____

_____

Conflict and Its Causes

It's clear that Kiko and Julia are having a **conflict**, or a disagreement. Conflict generally happens when people have different goals or interests. This causes the individuals to clash. On a team, conflict occurs when:

- Team members do not have clear direction about what they are supposed to do.
- Team members don't keep commitments.
- Team members don't communicate well with each other.
- Team members put their personal goals ahead of the team's goals.

Teams that plan well, have trust, and involve all members when making decisions are less likely to have conflict. However, most teams experience some conflict at some point. When conflict does occur, steps must be taken to resolve it. In this chapter, you will discover ways of resolving team conflict.

Conflict is a natural part of life.

> ➤ **Team Builder**

In the space below, describe a conflict that you have been involved in. What was the cause of this conflict?

_____

_____

_____

_____

We Can Work It Out

Paul took Kiko and Julia aside. "For the team's sake, are you willing to work out this problem?" he asked.

The two girls agreed. "OK," said Paul. "I want to lead this discussion. Here are the rules. No name calling. No interrupting. Our goal is to identify the problem and then solve it. Agreed?"

Again, the girls nodded.

"Julia, tell me what the problem is as you see it," continued Paul.

"Well," said Julia. "The team members gave us money to buy a tree for today's celebration. Kiko and I were supposed to buy it together. Instead, she went off and bought it herself!"

"That's right," said Kiko. "But, I went alone because Julia was late, and I was afraid that the store would close."

Julia made a face. "I couldn't help it. The bus was late. A good friend would have waited for me."

Paul held up his hands. "So, we have two different opinions. Julia, you thought it was important that you buy the tree together. Kiko, you thought it was more important to get to the store before it closed. Is that right?"

The girls nodded.

"What could be done to make you feel better?" asked Paul.

Julia spoke first. "I want Kiko to apologize for going without me," she said.

"OK," said Kiko, "As long as you admit I had to leave to get the tree in time."

How would you help Kiko or Julia resolve their differences?

"OK," replied Julia. "I admit that."

"Then I guess I apologize," said Kiko.

Paul smiled. "If everything is OK, let's get on with the celebration!"

Steps in Resolving Team Conflict

Paul was able to help Julia and Kiko work out their conflict. Teams often use these five basic steps to resolve conflict:

Step 1: Act Right Away. When any team member feels or sees conflict on the team, action must be taken immediately. Conflict almost never goes away by itself. The longer it exists, the worse it becomes. In some cases, team members can take action to resolve the conflict themselves. However, it's often wise to involve a third person. This person can guide the discussion and provide a different point of view.

A third party who helps solve problems is called a mediator.

Step 2: Set Discussion Rules. Everyone agrees on basic rules of behavior such as:

- Have respect for each other.
- Allow each person to speak without interruption.
- Be committed to solving the problem.
- Listen to each other.
- Focus on the problem, not the person.
- Focus on team goals, not personal issues.

Step 3: Figure Out the Problem. Many times, the people involved in a conflict are not really sure what the conflict is all about. They are too angry, upset, or frustrated to think clearly. The third person should ask questions and figure out what has gone wrong. It helps if the person states the problem from the two different points of view.

Paul did this when he said, "So, we have two different opinions. Julia, you thought it was important that you buy the tree together. Kiko, you thought it was more important to get to the store on time. Is that right?"

Step 4: Brainstorm Ways to Solve the Problem. Not all conflicts are solved as easily as Julia and Kiko's. It helps to brainstorm all of the possible solutions. The more creative the solutions, the better. For example, Paul might have suggested that Julia be allowed to plant the tree at the celebration. This way she would feel as if she had done her part.

Step 5: Choose a Solution that Works For Everyone. It is important that each person involved agrees that the solution chosen is the *best* solution. Without this agreement, conflict will still exist.

➤ Team Builder

Complete this activity with two classmates. One person should act as the team leader. The other two people take the role of Team Members A and B. Pretend that the two team members have approached the team leader with a conflict. Their job is to design a sign for the ice cream booth at the fair. Team Member A says that since she is the best artist, she should be allowed to paint the sign. Team Member B feels that he is the better artist and should paint the sign. Act out the situation with the team leader trying to resolve the conflict. Remember to use the steps outlined in the previous section.

1. Describe what occurred in the discussion. What was the outcome?

_____

➤ Dream Team Rules

Imagine you are starting a dream team. You decide to begin by drafting the team rules. Use the previous exercises in this book to help write the rules. Record them below.

We, the Dream Team, will use the following rules to guide our words and actions in the following areas:

1. Team Planning: _____

_____

_____

2. Team Trust: _____

_____

_____

3. Team Decisions: _____

_____

_____

4. Resolving Team Conflict: _____

_____

_____

Chapter Summary

- Conflict occurs when people disagree. Conflict happens when team members are not sure of their responsibilities; don't keep their commitments; don't communicate openly, or put their personal goals ahead of the team goals.
- Helpful steps in resolving conflicts are: act right away, set discussion rules, figure out the problem, brainstorm solutions, and choose the solution that all parties agree is best.
- When working to resolve conflict, people should: use a third person when needed, act with respect, avoid interruptions, be committed to solving the problem, focus on the problem rather than the person, and focus on team goals.

Chapter Review

Words to Know

Using complete sentences, write a definition of the word **conflict**.

_____

_____

About Resolving Team Conflict

Answer each question in the space provided.

1. Why is it important that team members act immediately when they discover conflict? _____

_____

2. Why is it important for the people involved in a conflict to feel that the chosen solution is the best solution? _____

_____

Getting Personal

Take a few minutes to review the chapters in this book. Identify the three most important things that you have learned from this book.

1. _____

2. _____

3. _____

Team Building

Words to Know

Match each word on the left to its meaning on the right. Write the correct letter in the space provided.

_____ **1.** accomplish

_____ **2.** approval

_____ **3.** brainstorm

_____ **4.** communicate

_____ **5.** conflict

_____ **6.** consensus

_____ **7.** criticize

_____ **8.** commitment

_____ **9.** majority

_____ **10.** outcomes

_____ **11.** progress

_____ **12.** purpose

_____ **13.** resolve

_____ **14.** team

_____ **15.** trust

_____ **16.** volunteer

_____ **17.** vote

a. to express a choice

b. to make fun of, or to judge

c. to achieve

d. agreement

e. people working together toward a common purpose

f. offer many ideas

g. to rely on or have confidence in

h. to send and receive messages

i. act of agreeing or giving consent to

j. to offer services free of charge or of one's own free will

k. disagreement due to different goals or interests; to clash

l. a promise to do something

m. the things you want to achieve

n. goal or objective

o. greater part or larger number

p. to move towards a goal

q. to work out or solve

About Team Building

Answer each question in the space provided.

1. Identify four things that help teams work well.

_____

_____

_____

_____

2. Describe the three parts of a team plan.

_____

_____

_____

3. What are three ways of building team trust?

_____

_____

_____

4. What do you think is the best way for a team to make a decision. Why?

_____

_____

_____

5. Which idea presented in this book will you use the most? Explain why.

_____

_____

Glossary

accomplish (uh-KAHM-plish): to achieve, 8

approval: the act of agreeing or giving consent to, 19

brainstorming: offering many ideas, 31

commitment: to promise to do something, 35

communicate: to send and receive messages, 33

conflict: disagreement due to different goals or interests; to clash, 54

consensus (kuhn-SEN-suhs): agreement, 44

criticize: to make fun of, or to judge, 31

majority: the greater part or larger number, 44

outcomes: the things you want to achieve, 22

progress: to move toward a goal, 24

purpose: goal or objective, 6

resolve (ri-ZAHLV): to work out or solve, 10

team: two or more people who work together toward a common goal, 6

trust: to rely on or have confidence in, 30

volunteer (vahl-uhn-TEER): to offer services free of charge or of one's own free will, 19

vote: to express a choice, 44